Vision Real

By Donald A. Peart

Vision Real Copyright © 2006 Donald A. Peart

ISBN: 978-0-9702301-8-8

Edition: September 2022

Cover Design by Donald Peart Jr.

Acknowledgement

Thanks to our Lord Jesus Christ for being my/our Lord, King, Savior, Baptizer and for His Holy Spirit that He has freely given us; "for it seemed good to the Holy Spirit…" for me to author this book.

Contents

The Vision 1

Straight-footed Vision 7

The Vision is for the Congregation 23

The Great Vision 29

The Vision Will Speak at the End 37

His Vision Personified 43

Tell the Vision to no One? 49

Eagle Flight 57

The Vision

Hebrews 10:37, KJV: For yet a little while, and **he that shall come will come, and will not tarry.**

Habakkuk 2:3, KJV: **For the vision** *is yet for an appointed time, but at the end it shall speak, and not lie: though it tarry, wait for it; because it will surely come, it will not tarry.*

The Lord's vision is one. There are many visions among the sons and daughters of God. However, the Lord has only one Vision. The Vision of God is primarily a "He." The phrase cited above in Hebrews 10:37 was quoted from the book of Habakkuk 2:3, also cited above.

The "it," in Habakkuk 2:3, is translated as a "He" in the book of Hebrews 10:37. In fact, the word "vision" in Habakkuk 2:3 is a masculine noun in the Hebrew text. Thus, in Habakkuk 2:3, the "it" is referring to the "masculine" vision, which is called "He" in Hebrews. The "He" is Jesus.

Becoming like Jesus is the vision, and this vision must become "real," or personified in His saints. All vision must be summed up in Him. A logical question is what is the meaning of Jesus' being the vision? There are many definitions for vision.

Vision could mean a dream, revelation, image, idea, and mental picture. The definition for "vision" in Habakkuk 2:3 as supplied by the Strong's Concordance is "sight (mental)," "to contemplate (with pleasure)," "to gaze at mentally," "a dream, revelation, or oracle."

Thus, when the redeemed daughters of God and the redeemed sons of God impart "vision" to the people, what kind of mental picture are they releasing in the people of God? Are they giving the people of God a "mental sight" of Jesus?

Or are they imparting the mental sight of another vision? What mental sight of Jesus should the saints see? The vision of God is to see believers of all races and cultures actualize the united and/or completed Christ-like character.

Daniel 10:5-6, NKJV: [5]I lifted my eyes and looked, and behold, a certain man clothed in linen, whose waist was girded with gold of Uphaz! [6]His body was like beryl, his face like the appearance of lightning, his eyes like torches of fire, his arms, and feet like burnished bronze in color, and the sound of his words like the voice of a multitude.

Daniel saw a **"certain man"** in Daniel 10:5. By interpolation, this "man" could be Gabriel (lit., Man of God, or Man-God). He is also an apostolic angel (Luke 1:19; 26). This "certain man" could also be compared to the "Son of man" that John saw in Revelation 1:12-16.

*Revelation 1:12-16, NKJV: [12]Then I turned to see the voice that spoke with me. And having turned I saw seven golden lampstands, [13]and in the midst of the seven lampstands **One like the Son of Man,** clothed with a garment down to the feet and girded about the chest with a golden band. [14]His head and hair were white like wool, as white as snow, and His eyes like a flame of fire; [15]His feet were like fine brass, as if refined in a furnace, and His voice as the sound of many waters; [16]He had in His right hand seven stars, out of His mouth went a sharp two-edged sword, and His countenance was like the sun shining in its strength.*

In Daniel, the "certain man" had "gold" around his waist. In Revelation, the "Son of Man" had a "golden band" around his chest. The men in Daniel and Revelation have "fire" in their eyes; so, does Jesus, as indicated in Revelation 2:18. They both have brass or bronze feet. One's face was like lightning[1] while the other's face was like the sun, and so on. My point is this; the "certain man" in Daniel has meaning relative to the Church's vision of Jesus as the Son of Man. Daniel called the man he saw "a certain man." "Certain" is defined in the Hebrew properly as "united" (see Strong's Concordance). Thus, this "certain man" is a "united" or corporate man created from all nations (Revelation 7; Ephesians 2). In other words, it is a group of diverse people "united" **as one man**. This united man or one new man made of Jews and Gentiles are transformed to be like the glorified Jesus as a "united" body of believers.

*Ezra 3:1, NKJV: And when the seventh month had come, and the children of Israel were in the cities, the people gathered together **as one (lit., united) man** to Jerusalem*

*Nehemiah 8:1, NKJV: Now all the people gathered **together as one (lit., united)** in the open square....*

*Ephesians 2:11-15, NKJV: [11]Therefore remember that you, once Gentiles in the flesh--who are called Uncircumcision by what is called the Circumcision made in the flesh by hands — [12]that at that time you were without Christ, being aliens from the commonwealth of Israel and strangers from the covenants of promise, having no hope and without God in the world. [13]But now in Christ Jesus you who once were far off have been brought near by the blood of Christ. [14]For He Himself is our peace, who has made both one, and has broken down the middle wall of separation, [15]having abolished in His flesh the enmity, ... so as to create in Himself **one new man** from the two, thus making peace.*

---

[1] The Hebrew word for lightning used in Daniel 10:6 is BaRaQ, which is defined in Strong's as: lightning, a gleam, a flashing sword, to lighten

The mature Church made of Jews and Gentiles is "one **new man.**" The mature in the Church is a "united man" that looks/acts like Jesus. There is the "general assembly" and there is the "Church of the firstborn" ("firstborn" is masculine plural in the Greek, see Hebrews 12:22).

These "firstborns" are the "first" who have become "united" as "one" into the exact image "like" the Son of Man. Daniel called the picture of the united man that he saw a "vision."

Daniel 10:5; 7-8, NKJV: *⁵I lifted my eyes and looked, and behold, a* ***'united'*** *man clothed in linen, whose waist was girded with gold of Uphaz! …. ⁷And I, Daniel, alone saw the* ***vision,*** *for the men who were with me did not see the* ***vision;*** *but a great terror fell upon them, so that they fled to hide themselves. ⁸Therefore I was left alone when I saw this* ***great vision,*** *and no strength remained in me; for my vigor was turned to frailty in me, and I retained no strength.*

The "vision" that Daniel saw includes the "united man" (as previously discussed). This is significant. This "man" that Daniel saw also had the **"likeness** of a man" (Daniel 10:18).

"Likeness" is the same word used by God when He called the Tabernacle of Moses a "pattern" (Numbers 8:4). Thus, this "man" is a "pattern." Saying it another way, this man is a mirror pattern of Jesus, glorified.

Vision in the verses above is defined as "mirror" by Strong's Dictionary. Thus, the "vision" is a "mirror" or a "pattern" of a "united man." In other words, the "mirror" of vision can only reflect what is "real." Vision is a mirror.

Vision is a pattern. The bodily reality of vision is the "truth." Daniel's vision pointed to a group of people who would become the very "truth" of the mirror Daniel saw. They will become the "completed man" by imaging the "pattern" of Jesus.

*Acts 12:9, NKJV: So, he went out and followed him, and did not know that what was done by the angel was **real**,[2] but **thought** he was seeing a **vision**.*

*Acts 12:9, KJV: And he went out, and followed him; and **knew** not that it was **true** which was done by the angel; but **thought** he saw a **vision**.*

Peter distinguished between "vision" and "truth" in Acts 12:9. The angel came to rescue him from apparent death. Peter "thought he was seeing a vision." However, the apparent vision "was real," or "true." Vision is not the very "truth," so to speak. Allow me to explain.

"Truth" literally means not to be hidden or not concealed. Thus, "a vision" (in its purest sense) is also something hidden or concealed. "Reality" or "truth" is that which is not hidden. The vision Daniel saw was "not the very image of the things" (Hebrews 10:1). The vision of the "united man" is a picture, pattern, or mirror of an actual body of believers who will personify the vision.

In other words, the "mirror pattern" will not be hidden forever. The reality of a group of people becoming the "completed man" will be unveiled. It will become reality or truth in the "Church of the firstborns" ("first" to "produce" the "reality" of a "completed man" (Hebrews 12:23; Ephesians 4:13)).

---

[2] Greek., alethes, NU text and Majority Texts

*Ephesians 4:13, NKJV: Till we all come to the unity of the faith and of the knowledge of the Son of God, to **a perfect (lit., complete) man,** to the measure of the stature of the fullness of Christ.*

"The unity of the faith" is related to the "united man," which is also related to the "prefect (lit., complete) man." The Church will not be united until her vision of the Son becomes one. Scattered vision causes a fragmented man.

The body of Christ must be united into one new man. In the words of Ezra and Nehemiah, we must be as "one man." In the words of Paul concerning "both" (Jews and Gentiles) God has made them "one…" (We are "completed into one" (see Greek definitions in John 17:23).

We are united into one Man — Jesus. "[We] are complete in Him" (Colossians 2:10a). The vision becoming a reality is the united Church becoming like the Son.

Straight-footed Vision

Galatians 2:11-14, NKJV: [11]*Now when Peter had come to Antioch, I withstood him to his face, because he was to be blamed;* [12]*for before certain men came from James, he would eat with the Gentiles; but when they came, he withdrew and separated himself, fearing those who were of the circumcision.* [13]*... so that even Barnabas was carried away with their hypocrisy.* [14]*But when I saw that they were not* **straightforward** *(Gk.:* **straight-footed**[3]*) about the truth of the gospel.*

Ezekiel 1:5-7, KJV: [5]*Also out of the midst thereof came the likeness of four living creatures...*[7]*And their feet were* **straight feet**...

Jesus has straight-feet. His feet is also shod and prepared with the gospel of peace (Ephesians 2:15). The same has to be true for Jesus' ministers.

A visionary that understands and implements "the truth of the gospel" that all ethnics are to work together in Christ without "boundaries" is a "straight-footed" thinker. I believe one of the most divisive issues in the Church of today, relative to God's vision of one new united man, is race and/or culture[4] mingled in the sinful nature. God is looking for a Church who can function as a unit with diversity.

There is no such entity as a "Black Church." This mind set is a form of chauvinism by the Black people who use this phrase. There is no such thing as a "White Church."

You may have a Church made up of Chinese, but there is no such thing as a "Chinese Church." Practices of prejudices relative to

---

[3] See Strong's Concordance or Vines Expository Dictionary
[4] Another, certainly historic, divisive issue is doctrinal differences

brothers and sisters of the Heavenly Jerusalem are not the "straight-footed…truth of the gospel." Some Churches are built upon a cast system based on race. Some of the "Korean Church's" leaders are based mostly on a cast system within their race. Thus, any vision of integration by any other race into a leadership position is next to impossible. As indicated earlier, Paul taught that separation from other races as not walking with a "straight foot" (Galatians 2:14). Paul did not mind "Niger" (lit., "Black") laying hands on him in Acts 13:1.

Prejudging hinders the fulfillment of God's vision of developing a united holy nation made up of many "ethnic" groups. Paul states that God's nation made up of many ethnic groups is the mystery that was hidden from other generations "by which, when you read, you may understand my [Paul's] knowledge in the mystery of Christ) …that the **Gentiles (lit., Ethnics)** should be fellow heirs, of the **same body**…" (Ephesians 3:4-6, NKJV).

Church segregation is unacceptable. One of the reasons is: vision is skewed by respecting persons based on race. Thus, it is damaging to let race be an issue relative to serving God and fellowshipping with one another.

There are some "Black Churches" who will not submit to the leadership of a "White Church." There are "White Churches" that will fellowship with "Blacks" or a "Black Church." Yet, most of the time, it is in the context of the "Black Church" being in a student role.

Then, there are some Messianic Churches that want all believers to observe their traditions (contrast Acts 15). Jesus is not building the "Black" Church, "White" Church, "Korean" Church, etc.! Jesus is building His Church which includes all races. The Church should not separate herself by emphasizing "endless" racial pedigrees (I Timothy 1:4, Hebrews 7:3).

These things ought not to be so! Getting caught up in "genealogies (race and/or gene) ... causes disputes rather than godly edification (NU, M Texts: God's dispensation)" (I Timothy 1:4). The Church is diverse, made up of Jew and Gentiles. Noah, whether he was Black or White, had "Shem (Jews), Ham (Blacks, or "people of colors"[5] as defined by some) and Japheth (Whites). Our "Greater Noah" – Jesus – also has children from all continuums of colors.

Thus, prejudices must be eliminated from man's "mental sight" (vision). The Bible calls those who walk without intolerances as "straight footed." Paul had to remind Peter that Peter had to be "straight-footed about the truth of the gospel." That means, when prejudices are eliminated, different races can "eat with the (other) ethnics" who are part of God's Church.

Galatians 2:11-14, NKJV: [11]*Now when Peter had come to Antioch, I withstood him to his face, because he was to be blamed;* [12]*for before certain men came from James, he would eat with the Gentiles (lit., Ethnics); but when they came, he withdrew and separated himself, fearing those who were of the circumcision.* [13]*And the rest of the Jews also played the hypocrite with him, so that even Barnabas was carried away with their hypocrisy.* [14]*But when I saw that they were not* **straightforward (lit.; straight-footed)** *about the truth of the gospel.*

Ezekiel 1:4-7, KJV: [5]*Also out of the midst thereof came the likeness of four living creatures...*[7]*And their feet were* **straight feet.**

---

[5] It seems to me all the peoples of the earth have color, races have color white is a color, yellow is a color, brown id a color

Some of the Jews before Christ were a people filled with separatism (John 4:9). In Acts 10, God had to address Peter's prejudgments, and in Galatians 2, Paul also had to address Peter's narrow-mindedness. Peter did not want to eat with the "ethnics."

Today, we call it Blacks who do not fellowship with Whites; Korean who does not develop genuine relationship with Whites; and some Jewish believers who are "separated" unto themselves. The sad thing is these are saints from the same mother (the heavenly Jerusalem) and from the same father (Abraham) who will not even eat together.) Paul then stated that if we put a difference between races, it is considered "hypocrisy" and "not (being) straight-footed." In other words, God considers a prejudiced person "crooked-footed." Most of the church world is "not straight-footed." The so called "Black Church," the "White Church," the "Asian Church," the "Messianic Jewish Church," and so on is "not straight-footed." When people say, "Black Church," "White Church," etc., it makes it emphasizes man's vision of color. Thus, we make the Church's vision of today "crooked."

This kind of behavior is opinionated against God's vision of "one new man" made up of "both" Jews and Ethnics. When we understand that the Church is made up of Jews, Blacks, Whites, and Asians, then the purchased possession become God's. We can be "straight-footed" by having true fellowship with other believers.

I am not saying that we must be in each other's faces all the time. What I am saying is: let there be genuine relationship. Relationships affect how we relate to God on His Throne. If we cannot walk "straight-footed," we do not dwell in the Most Holy Place — the Throne Room of God.

The Cherubs that Ezekiel saw also have "straight feet" (Ezekiel 1:7). The Cherubs carry the Throne of God (Ezekiel 1:26). If you can receive it, "the cherubim of glory overshadowing the mercy seat" are also symbols of a "straight-footed" Church united with Jesus — the personification of the Mercy Seat (or the Throne).

Peter, for a time, did not walk with "straight feet." He did not publicly show mercy toward those who look and eat differently from him; and he had to be corrected by another apostle (Paul) (Galatians 2:14).

The point is this: Churches who are not "straight footed" are hindering the positive affect of God's Mercy Throne in their ministry. The Throne of God is the place of grace and mercy (Hebrews 4:16); and "straight feet" supports the flow of God's grace and mercy to all races of diverse cultures and colors. In fact, around God's Throne is a "rainbow" which is made up of many colors, and His beauty is seen through all colors.

Ezekiel 1:26;2 8, NKJV: ²⁶*And above the firmament over their heads was the likeness of a throne… * ²⁸*Like the appearance of a **rainbow** in a cloud on a rainy day, so was the appearance of the brightness all around it. This was the appearance of the likeness of the glory of the LORD.*

Revelation 4:2-3, NKJV: ²*Immediately I was in the Spirit; and behold, a throne set in heaven, and One sat on the throne.* ³*…; and there was a rainbow around the throne, in appearance like an emerald.*

The many-colored rainbow show God's love for color. Am I not competent because of my color? Do I not have God's revelation because of my color? Do I not have the true Spirit of God because of my color? I do have the Spirit of Revelation regardless of my race! I am competent (skillful) in the Words of Righteousness!

I do have the Holy (lit., Clean) Spirit of Jesus. God's wisdom is made of "many colors" (see Greek definitions for "manifold" in Ephesians 3:10). Anyone who does not walk with "straight feet," the Bible says that example is "not … the truth of the gospel" (Galatians 2:14, NKJV).

In other words, walking with a partisan lifestyle is like walking in a lie—the opposite of the truth. Prejudices are beliefs in false visions, false fates, and suspicions. The only way this issue will be dealt with is when it is addressed publicly like Paul did. In our vernacular, this means address biases by open dialogs. It is also important to note that Paul is of the same race as Peter.

It will take men and women of like races to censure their own race concerning "the truth of the gospel"—there are to be no prejudices. We all must walk with "straight-feet" like Jesus. We must become like the Cherubim of glory—having "straight feet," Paul also walked with "straight-feet." He had an apostolic vision to and for the ethnics. Eventually, Peter was also made straight in his understanding. Peter, through revelation from the Lord, became one of the first whose "vision" had to be **straightened**. He became one of the first to walk in "straight-footed" vision. He was one of the first to minister salvation to the "ethnics."

He was, originally, afraid like most people today. He had phobias and suspicions about being defiled by other races. It is a sick vision to despise your fellow brothers and sisters as being inferior or what Peter called "common or unclean."

God had to deal with Peter's crooked feet in a vision, and then Peter had to walk according to the "straight" vision. Peter's vision became a reality. The apparent "wild beasts"[6] and "creeping things" are "cleansed" people.

They are not "common." And yes there will be opposition from your fellow race for walking straight-footed with other races! However, God will honor straight-footed ministers by bearing witness with His Holy Spirit (Acts 10:28; 44). The Lord is for peace, and He will open the eyes of those who are still "not straight-footed" Listen to Peter whose feet were straightened.

Acts 11:1-18, NKJV: [1]Now the apostles and brethren who were in Judea heard that the Gentiles had also received the word of God. [2]And when Peter came up to Jerusalem, those of the circumcision contended with him, [3]saying, "You went into uncircumcised men and ate with them!" [4]But Peter explained it to them in order from the beginning, saying: [5]"I was in the city of Joppa praying; and in a trance, I saw a vision, an object descending like a great sheet, let down from heaven by four corners; and it came to me. [6]When I observed it intently and considered, I saw four-footed animals of the earth, wild beasts, creeping things, and birds of the air. [7]And I heard a voice saying to me, 'Rise, Peter; kill and eat.' [8]But I said, 'Not so, Lord! For nothing common or unclean has at any time entered my mouth.' [9]But the voice answered me again from heaven, 'What God has cleansed you must not call common.' [10]Now this was done three times, and all were drawn up again into heaven. [11]At that very moment, three men stood before the house where I was, having been sent to me from Caesarea. [12]Then the Spirit told me to go with them, doubting nothing. Moreover, these six brethren accompanied me, and we entered the man's house. [13]And he told us how he had seen an angel standing in his house, who said to

---

[6]A modern-day example of this is South Africa's apartheid that was also built upon calling Black Africans "beast."

him, 'Send men to Joppa, and call for Simon whose surname is Peter, *14who will tell you words by which you and all your household will be saved.'* *15"And as I began to speak, the Holy Spirit fell upon them, as upon us at the beginning.* *16Then I remembered the word of the Lord, how He said, 'John indeed baptized with water, but you shall be baptized with the Holy Spirit.'* *17"If therefore God gave them the same gift as He gave us when we believed on the Lord Jesus Christ, who was I that I could withstand God?"* *18When they heard these things they became silent; and they glorified God, saying, "Then God has also granted to the Gentiles repentance to life."*

The vision of God is as He showed it to Peter. He has cleansed all believers by the same blood and has given them the same Holy (lit., Clean) Spirit. There is no difference. God is still calling a people who were not formerly near to Him (Isaiah 55:5; 1 Peter 2:10). Do not "withstand God" by intolerance.

Jesus is "straight-footed." One of His apostles was a Canaanite—a non-Jew (Matt 10:4a). He expects His Bride, the Church to be "straight-footed." The vision of one nation made up out of many nations is still one of God's goals. I like the motto from the Jamaica, West Indies, "Out of many, one people." The vision of a corporate Christ on earth is real.

With that said, I thought if fit to **add** the next chapter ("God Gene"), an excerpt (quoted) from one of my books, titled *You Exist! (Understanding Your Identity),* after reformatting this book and reading the previous chapter on straight-footed vision.

God Gene

Genesis 1:26-27: *26And God said, let us make man in **our image,** after **our likeness** …. 27So God created man in **his image**, in the image of God created he him ….*

*Titus 3:5: Not by works of righteousness which we have done, but according to his mercy **he saved us,** by the washing of **regeneration,** and renewing **of the Holy Ghost.***

All humans are created in the image of God with the gene of God. When we accept Jesus as Savior, the Holy Spirit also "regenerates" us. That is, we are "regened" through the Spirit, in spirit. One of the apparent reasons Jesus taught that we are not to call a brother a "fool"("empty-one") is because we are all made in God's image; and we have His similitude (His gene).

Since man is made in the image of God, if we curse a fellow man, by calling him a fool ("empty-one"); we are calling God's gene empty. God is not empty! Jesus is the wisdom of God; and His "variegated wisdom" is in His Church, made up of Jews and non-Jews!

*Mathew 5:22: But I say unto you … whosoever shall say to his brother … you **'empty-one'** shall be **'liable'** of **'Gehenna'** fire.*

*James 3:8-9: [8]But the tongue can no man tame; [it is] an unruly evil, full of deadly poison. [9]Therewith we bless God, even the Father; and therewith we curse **men, which are made after the similitude of God.***

Every race is exemplary of the image of God, or "the similitude of God." Every race has gene from God. There is no "difference between a Jew and a 'non-Jew.'" We all were created by the same God. We all answer to the "same" Lord. There are no "prejudices" with God.

*Romans 10:12: For there is **no difference** between the Jew and the **Greek**; for **the same Lord over all is** rich unto all that call upon him.*

*Genesis 1:27: So, God created man in **his image**, in the **image of God** created he him ….*

A Black man is created with the gene of God. An East Asian man is created with the gene of God. An Indian man is created with the gene of God, A White man is created with the gene of God, and a Jew is created with the gene of God, and so on. So, God must have various colors of genes in Him.

It appears to me that the problem is not with genes, the problem lays in which God we serve. There is only one God, the Father of our Lord Jesus Christ. God was not prejudice in the Old Testament, as some assert. God took exception to people who worshipped idols and served other gods; and God still takes exception to other gods (Revelation 9:20-21).

Thus, to curse a Black man is to curse God's color. To curse a Spaniard and Latino is to curse God's color. To curse any colors of man (black, yellow, white, red, and brown) is to curse God's gene. As we previously read, James, Jesus' brother, stated this truth some two thousand years ago; saying if we curse man who is made in the similitude of God, we are cursing God. Thus, humans should be careful not to make assertion concerning genealogy.

*1 Timothy 1:4: Neither give heed to fables and **endless genealogies,** which minister questions, rather than godly edifying which is in faith.*

There are some that make a big splash concerning racial purity and racial inferiority, including some Jews. Yet, in every race there exist non-productive people who have identity issues. This dispute of identity issues is not related to certain race, or people of so-called mixed backgrounds! All this position does is "minister questions." Yet, if you look at the lineage of Jesus (a Jew), we will quickly see that His genealogy is mixed. So, maybe this "will 'muzzle' the ignorance 'imprudence' of men" concerning the so called "purity" of certain gene.

Ezekiel 16:3 indicates that the Father of the Jewish race was an Amorite (a non-Jew). Deuteronomy 26:5 defined this "Amorite" as an "Aramaean." Ezekiel also stated that the Jewish race mother was a Hittite (modern day Turkey); and Hittite, by definition, means "terror." In Jesus lineage was also Rahab, a Canaanite prostitute.

She mothered Boaz, which makes Boaz a half Jew. Boaz, in turn, married another non-Jew, a Moabite called Ruth. Boaz and Ruth were the great grandparents of David. So, what gene was David made of? In addition, Solomon, David's son by murder and deception, came from the wife of Uriah, a Hittite (a Turk), one of David's mighty men. So, what was this "Turk" doing in Israel's army, if God is against certain gene?

*John 1:12: But as many as **received him**, to them he gave '**authority**' to become the **offspring'** of God, to them that believe on his name:*

It seems to me that the God we serve also defines our gene and identity based the God we serve! Those who "believe in Jesus" is given the "authority" to "exist out of their 'I's'" to become offspring of God. Therefore, was Uriah's God, the God of Israel? Uriah was a Turk, yet he was one of David's mighty men in the army of Israel, who fought under the banner of the God of Israel.

Abraham, Caleb, Rahab, Ruth, were of various races; but what made them "the Israel of God" is that they believed and served the same God; the God of Israel! The same God of Jesus is the same God of the Israel! The same God of Israel is the same God of the Church. Through Jesus, the Church is now a "holy nation," a new nation, with sons of God who are peacemakers!

And finally, Jesus was conceived by the Holy Spirit through Mary and through the lineage I briefly listed above. That is, Jesus had a checkered lineage and gene. So being mixed race does not disqualify you to be used by God or called is offspring. Jesus was qualified with of His history!

Being a mixed race does not make one inferior, as some have tried to use the phrase "mixed multitude" used Exodus 12:28 and Nehemiah 13:13 to judge multiracial backgrounds. The phrase "mixed multitude" in the verses just cited is literally translated as "Arabians." Arabians received salvation of the outpouring of the Holy

Spirit in Acts, Chapter 2. Thus, being black or mixed black does not make one inferior. A "mixed race" background did not make Jesus inferior; and it did not disqualify Him to be the Christ.

On the contrary, your history is part of your identity. Here is my point, mixed genes do not thwart your identity. People who debate "endless genealogy" only "generate questions." So, how do we build identity? Identity is found in the Father, God. Let me explain.

Jesus, at age twelve (12) showed no sign of a lack of "ego" (self-esteem, self-confidence, self-importance, etc.); and understood His "existence" to be in and from His Father in heaven. His lack of an earthy father (as some experience today with vacated dads) did not result in His identity being shattered. In other words, Jesus understood that His identity is found in His invisible Father, God, and not necessarily in His stepfather. With the understanding that I am not saying that His stepdad, Joseph, did not impart good things to Jesus. Joseph was a "just" man (Matthew 1:19).

So, at age twelve, Jesus stayed back at the temple speaking with teachers and scribes. When Jesus' stepfather and His natural mother became aware that He was not with the group, they went back to the temple area to look for Jesus. After they found Him, they questioned Him about His whereabouts, and His response at age twelve was profound. Jesus at age twelve (12) understood His spiritual identity to be that of His Heavenly Father and not that of His earthly stepfather. He made it clear who is His real Father is and identified with His Father in the heavens.

Luke 2:48-49: [48]*And when they saw him, they were amazed; and* **his mother said** *unto him, Son, why have you thus dealt with us? Behold,* **your father and I** *have sought you sorrowing.* [49]*And he said unto them, how is it that you sought me? Know you not that I must be* **'in the things of my Father?'**

People of the whole habitable earth who are confused about their identity because of a lack of earthly father and mother, need to know this truth. God, the Father, is the source of your identity, not just you race or ethnicity. You have God genes! God is your Father!

Note: Jesus did not necessarily identify with his earthly stepfather, His identity was with His Heavenly Father. *"Behold,* **your father** *and I have sought you sorrowing.* [49]*And he said unto them, how is it that you sought me? Know you not that I must be 'in the things of* **my Father?'"**

Titus 3:5: Not by works of righteousness which we have done, but according to his mercy **he saved us,** *by the washing of* **regeneration,** *and renewing* **of the Holy Ghost.**

John 3:6: That which is born of the flesh is flesh; and that which is born of the Spirit is spirit.

We also were "regenerated" when we were washed through water baptism and the baptism of the Holy Spirit. You are spirit, you have a soul, and you live in a body. God gave us His gene and "regened" us into His image and His likeness by the Holy Spirit. If you have accepted Jesus as Savior and Lord, you were connected to the forty-second generation of Jesus Christ. That is, God regened us into His generation and disconnected us from the generations of the world.

You exist! You are important. Your gene is just as good as anyone else. Allow God to mature you into one His many sons and daughters!

The Vision is for the Congregation

Habakkuk 2:3, KJV: For the vision is yet for an appointed time (or congregation), but at the end it shall speak, and not lie: though it tarry, wait for it; because it will surely come, it will not tarry.

Jesus is the vision. "The vision is ... for a congregation." Yes, the Hebrew word translated as "appointed time" is also translated "technically" as "the congregation" by Strong's Concordance, and in the Scriptures.[7]

It appears that most leaders have been guilty of having a vision for themselves. However, the vision of God is for the congregation. Very often, we use the term and hear the term "my vision." However, the vision should not be "my vision."

The vision should be "His vision" or 'the vision." It should be "'His' vision for the congregation." For most men and women who say they are of God, the vision appears to be for themselves. However, God's vision for the congregation was set forth in Ephesians 4:11-13.

Ephesians 4:11-13, NKJV: *11 And he gave some ...12for the equipping of the saints for the work of ministry, for the edifying (or, architecture, structure)[8] of the body of Christ, 13 till we all come to the unity of the faith and of the knowledge of the Son of God, to a perfect man, to the measure of the stature of the fullness of Christ.*

God's vision is for the whole body of Christ — the Congregation. The Vision of God is "for the equipping of the 'saints' for the

---

[7]See Exodus 27:21; 28:43, etc.; Strong's Concordance #4150 (Old Testament section)
[8]See Strong's Concordance New Testament #3619

work of the ministry." The vision for the congregation is for the "architecture" or "structure" of the "body of Christ" – not necessarily the construction of a natural building. The vision for the congregation is for "all to come to ...a perfect man...." Most have made the body of Christ a slave to their own vision, rather than implementing Jesus vision[9] for the congregation.

I remember in the early 1990s, I was in a building that housed a church. As I was there, the leader of the congregation continued and on about raising money for a building fund. That day, I went home very disturbed and asked God what is the true purpose of a church; because it was apparent to me that money for manmade buildings was preeminent in the vision of most.

To my excitement, the Lord replied through Paul's writing. Paul stated that his foremost practice was to preach "Christ in you (us)." The end of this practice is to "present every man perfect (lit., complete) in Christ" (see Colossians 1:28).

Colossians 1:28, NKJV: Him we preach, warning (lit., to put in mind) every man and teaching every man in all wisdom, that we may present every man perfect (lit., complete) in Christ Jesus.

When, I read this verse, the voice of the Holy Spirit said to me on the inside, "the goal of every man of God should be to present every man perfect (complete) in Christ," the purpose for the Church is not primarily for building natural buildings.

---

[9] Jesus vision is three (3) phased. (1) We are to attain to the same **faith** as the Son of God; (2) we are to attain to the same **knowledge** as the Son of God; (3) we are to attain to the **"'mature' man" (love)** as the Son of God is love personified (Ephesians 4:11-16)

There are so many incomplete people in the Congregation today because the emphasis is for a "worldly sanctuary"[10] instead of inward development. The focus is merchandising (which is linked to the mark of the beast). The focus of most is not for Christ being completed in the congregation.

Paul's goal (vision) for the Church was "warning" — literally, "putting [Christ] in the mind" of "every man," to the end that the congregation may be "perfect in Christ." Remember, I indicated in the first chapter that vision also means "mental sight." Thus, Paul's goal is to "put" the "sight" (vision) of Christ in the "mind" (mentality) of believers. The vision is for the congregation.

The congregation is not for men's personal visions. The vision is for becoming like the Son of Man in His "exact character!" Jesus glorified in His congregation is the vision! Leaders should "labor" to "form" Christ "in" the Church of Jesus" (Galatians 4:19).

*Galatians 4:19, NKJV: My little children, for whom I **labor [KJV "travail"]** in birth again until Christ is formed in you,*

The emphasis today is outward or worldly beauty. Contrarily, Paul's vision was for Christ to be formed "in" you. True apostles emphasize the "internal" reality of Christ, with the outward flowing of His character. It is not in what you exhibit (i.e., expensive garb, expensive building, and expensive cars).

According to the Scripture, fancy dress is marginalized to emphasize "meek and quiet spirit" in men and women. I say this with the understanding that God did indeed create a beautiful

---

[10]See the King James Version or the Greek text for Hebrews 9:1

earth for all to enjoy; and there is nothing wrong with dressing beautifully and creating beautiful surroundings. It is the incorrect "spirit' behind the emphasis of worldly beauty that misrepresents God.

1 Peter 3:3-4, KJV: ³Whose adorning let it not be that outward adorning (lit., worldliness) of plaiting the hair, and of wearing of gold, or of putting on of apparel; ⁴But let it be the hidden man of the heart, in that which is not corruptible, even the ornament of a meek and quiet (lit., to keep one's seat) spirit, which is in the sight of God of great price.

The vision of most today is to be dressed in an expensive car, to be dressed in the expensive house, and dressed in an expensive church building, and so on. Yet, there is no internal quietness and meekness. Many are so busy with external dress; they rarely take the time to "take a seat" in meekness. Their vision is all about the external. The balance to this is to enjoy life with the right attitude towards God; because the other extreme, austerity (strictness) in the name of religion may border on masochism.[11]

With that said, the apostolic vision does not emphasize the external. The vision of the apostles is for the perfecting of the internal state of the congregation. The Vision for the congregation is for inward completion in Christ — Christ must be "formed in [us]."

We must reach the "goal" of the "award" as outlined in Philippians 3:10-14. Like Christ, we must "form in" the congregation the "ability" to dominate in "all things that pertain to life and godliness (lit., good fear)" (2 Peter 1:3).

---

[11]Gratification gained from pain, deprivation, degradation, etc., inflicted or imposed on oneself

According to Paul, Christ is formed by "travailing in birth" for the saints. The vision of Christ is not formed by manmade items. One of the sins of today is leaders emphasizing the "work of their hands" (Revelation 9:20).

The emphasis should be the vision for the congregation, which is the reality of Christ being completed "in" the Congregation. This forming of Christ in us (the congregation) is to be done "without hands" (Hebrews 9:11; Colossians 2:11, Daniel 2); and is not to be measured by manmade visions. Travailing in prayer will cause the vision of Christ being formed in His congregation to become real.

The Great Vision

*Daniel 10:8, NKJV: Therefore, I was left alone when I saw this **great vision**, and no strength remained in me; for my vigor was turned to frailty in me, and I retained no strength.*

Jesus is the greatest vision (goal) that a person can ever attain to. In continuance, great vision, in the context of Daniel, Chapter 10, also includes envisioning (mirroring) the "pattern man" — the Christ (both head (Jesus, the Christ) and body (the body of Christ).

It is Jesus who is being "formed" in "His congregation" as we become a "united man" as Christ. Great vision is seeing the body of believers as Christ. The congregation is not the Christ. However, according to Paul, the body as a united whole "is Christ."

*1 Corinthians 12:12, NKJV: For **as the body is one** and has many members, but all the members of that one body, being many, are **one body, so also is Christ.***

*Daniel 10:5, NKJV: I lifted my eyes and looked, and behold, a **certain (lit., united) man** clothed in linen, whose waist was girded with gold of Uphaz!*

*Galatians 4:19, NKJV: My little children, for whom I labor in birth again until **Christ** is formed in you.*

*Daniel 10:18, NKJV: Then again, the one having the **likeness (lit., pattern) of a man** touched me and strengthened me.*

"Christ" is now "many members … all the members … are one body so also is Christ." This many members body is what Daniel called the "united man." The vision is "the Christ" being "formed" in His "many members" to manifest His glory in all the earth as "one man." Saying it another way, great vision is to see a "man" of believers who eventually becomes "united" to express His glory from the inside out. This is what the prophet called "great vision."

There is also a little more as to why Daniel called the vision of the united man great. It has to do with how the vision "affects" the beholder. The vision affected Daniel in what appears to be a strange way. The interesting thing is that all through the Scriptures, great vision affected other prominent men of God in the same way. There is an "affect" ("cause") of great vision, and there is an "effect" ("product") of great vision. Let us look at the "affect."

Daniel 10:8-9; 16, NKJV: ⁸Therefore I was left alone when I saw this great vision, and no strength remained in me; for my vigor was turned to frailty in me, and I retained no strength⸱ ⁹Yet I heard the sound of his words; and while I heard the sound of his words I was in a deep sleep on my face, with my face to the ground⸱⸱⸱ ¹⁶And …because of the vision my sorrows have overwhelmed me, and I have retained no strength

Great vision has an effect. These effects answer the questions of those who truly have a great vision from God. Thus, let us look at the effect of great vision as listed above.

Great vision causes the beholder "not to retain strength" (compare 2 Corinthians 12:10, last part). The beholder's "vigor" will be "turned to "frailty" or "sleep" (lit., to stupefy or to be stunned). Sleep may set in, and "overwhelming sorrow" because of great vision.

When a man or woman of God receives great vision from the Holy Spirit, there is an "effect" that is not necessarily an immediate positive effect. After Daniel saw the great vision, the first effect was weakness—he "retained no strength." That is strange! It would appear, strength should come from vision. However, the experience of Daniel indicates differently. This truth is also conveyed in the New Covenant, as referenced earlier.

2 Corinthians 12:1; 7-10, NKJV: ¹It is doubtless not profitable for me to boast. I will come to visions and revelations of the Lord: ⋯⁷And lest I should be exalted above measure by the abundance of the revelations, a thorn in the flesh was given to me, a messenger of Satan to buffet me, lest I be exalted above measure. ⁸Concerning this thing I pleaded with the Lord three times that it might depart from me. ⁹And He said to me, "My grace is sufficient for you, for My strength is made perfect in weakness." Therefore, most gladly I will rather boast in my infirmities, that the power of Christ may rest upon me. ¹⁰Therefore I take pleasure in infirmities, in reproaches, in needs, in persecutions, in distresses, for Christ's sake. For when I am weak, then I am strong.

Paul had visions and revelations, and the "effect" of his "abundance of the revelations" was "weakness." Great vision[12] or revelations will cause weakness. Why should we be weak relative to great vision or "abundant revelation?" The answer is: "[The Lord's] strength is made perfect in weakness." Our ego will not be able to take any credit; for it is God who is working through us to fulfill His vision (1 Corinthians 1:29).

---

[12]As indicated in the first chapter "vision" is also defined as "revelation" by Strong's Concordance.

Yet, there is a problem among some leaders. They are using their strength instead of the Lord's strength. I can hear the voice of some saying, "What is weakness, or how do I become weak?" One becomes weak by allowing God to give him/her God's vision. As for what is this "weakness" that Paul called a "thorn," and/or the "messenger (angel) of Satan?" I recommend reading 2 Corinthians 12.

Next, Daniel also experienced "frailty" of his "vigor" – "for my vigor (lit., grandeur, beauty, comeliness) was turned to frailty (lit., destructive) in me." This is a strong effect. Daniel's internal beauty was affected.

In other words, great vision or godly vision will "destroy" any hidden conceitedness about personal beauty that a person may possess. Daniel was good looking (Daniel 1:4). Yet, Daniel's beauty became "frail" in comparison to God's beautiful vision. God's vision destroys any worldly charm that may exist in the beholder of His vision. God's Vision is not built upon man's opinions of beauty. Daniel's "beauty" also became "destructive" when he saw the glory of the united man (see Daniel 10:5-6).

Man's beauty (grandeur) is always swallowed up by His righteous beauty that is imparted to us. In other words, the thing that brings people to their knees is a revelation of the glory (beauty) of Christ in His body (Revelation 1:12-13 w/Revelation 12:17). Hear the prophet's description of true beauty!

This united man had "gold" around his "waist" (waist points to the sex life, eating life and drinking life), "body like beryl (can point to Zebulon, God inhabiting His people through His Spirit), his face like the appearance (lit., pattern) of lightning (course and speed of the Spirit led cherubs), his eyes like torches of fire (he can search the kidneys and heart)" His "arms and feet like burnished bronze (prayer/worship that leads to judgment)."

Finally, in proof that the vision of this "certain man" is a "united man," the sound of his words is like the "voice of a multitude." The vision's "voice" is a "multitude" that becomes as "one man."

Thirdly, the vision caused Daniel to sleep. "Sleep" is defined as "to stun," "to stupefy." This means that great vision will make you look "dazed" at times. There are times that the vision of God is so overwhelming that it will cause "sleep."

Thus, God will be needed to lay his hands on that person to awake him/her out of the apparent stupor. John had a vision of one "like the Son of Man" (Revelation 1:13). The vision's effect on John was that John became "as dead"—"And when I saw Him, I fell at His feet as dead." Yet, it did not stop there.

"He [the Son of Man] laid His right hand on him" to strengthen him (see Revelation 1:17). Great vision will sometimes put a person into a sleep or as dead (compare Genesis 15:12). Why?

As indicated earlier, Jesus' strength is made perfect in our weakness. When vision makes us become as dead, the Lord will lay His right hand on us to impart His strength in us. This will enable us to see the complete vision and make His vision a reality. "Then again, the one having the likeness of a man touched me and strengthened me" (Daniel 10:18, NKJV).

Finally, great vision will sometimes cause "overwhelming sorrow." "And ...because of the vision my sorrows (lit., throe, mental pressure, to hinge, a messenger as constrained) have overwhelmed me..." (Daniel 10:16, NKJ).

Has God's vision for your life ever overwhelmed you? Has His vision for us to become like His uniquely begotten Son — Jesus — ever overwhelmed you with sorrow?

For most the answer is yes! It appears that we cannot attain to God's great vision. Yet, God expect us to become like His First Son — Jesus. Thus, this place of sorrow is good because it makes one wise to believe God's vision for his/her life.

Sorrow is not always negative. Sometimes sorrow is intended to produce a good result. The face of the heart is made better by sorrow.

*Ecclesiastes 7:3-4, KJV: [3]Sorrow is **better** than laughter: for by the sadness of the countenance the heart is made better. [4]The heart of the wise is in the house of mourning; but the heart of fools is in the house of mirth.*

An "effect" (result) of great vision is always good, even though the immediate "effect" (change) does not appear positive. A result of sorrow[13] is to "make the heart better."

Thus, even though Daniel went through a period of sorrow, the result was always better (Daniel 12:13). Vision may make us "mourn" today; however, our hearts will eventually be made better. The vision will complete in us the better heart that God desires to be a reality in us.

Remember great vision may cause sleep (Daniel 10:9). Great vision may cause a fall (Acts 9:4, Ezekiel 1:28, last part,

---

[13]Compare 2 Corinthians 7:10 where it is indicated: "the sorrow of God that works repentance to salvation," **not** "the sorrow of the world which works death" (suicide)

Revelation 1:17). Yet, remember that "The end of a thing is better than its beginning" (Ecclesiastes 7:8).

Realizing of vision is always better than the process of making the vision real. Beloved, God's vision is "great" for your life. Endure the apparent "contradiction." "For consider him that endured such contradiction of sinners against himself, lest ye be wearied and faint in your minds" (Hebrews 12:3, KJV). The great vision of God will be realized with Christ's glory manifesting in us and His glory breaking through our skin for all creation to see.

The Vision Will Speak at the End

Habakkuk 2:3, KJV: For the vision is yet for an appointed time, but at the end it shall speak, and not lie: though it tarry, wait for it; because it will surely come, it will not tarry.

The vision will eventually speak. This vision also does not lie. It is filled with the speech of faith and the spirit of faith. The question though is when? Habakkuk indicated that the vision would speak "at the end." This "end" has been sealed to those without the Holy Spirit and "the Word of God" for many generations.

Thus, there are several ways, biblically, to understand times[14] (plural) and seasons (plural) of the "end." Since the vision is Jesus — who is a person, I will begin by showing how the "end" is also linked to His Church — people.

1 Corinthians 10:11, NKJV: Now all these things happened to them as examples, and they were written for our admonition, on (Gk., eis, into) whom **the ends of the ages have come.**

Paul was writing to the Corinthians about lifestyle referring to what happened to the Israelites in the wilderness. He then summed up his discourse by indicating that the things that happened to the Israelites in the wilderness were "examples."

These "examples" were "written for our admonition...on (lit., into) whom the ends of the ages have come (lit., come down)." This is uncomplicated; the "ends (plural) of the ages (plural)

---

[14]Please refer to my book, The Last Hour, The First Hour, The Forty-second Generation

have come." However, the "ends" is linked "into" a living body called the Church.

The phrase "have come" is present perfect tense in the Greek.[15] This means that the "ends of the ages" already happened. Yes! The "ends" have "come down" already. The "ends of the ages" will also consummate at the end of these ages. However, the point I wanted to make here is that "the end" is linked with something happening "into" the believers. Peter also indicated that the saints are the ones "hasting the coming of the day of God."

*2 Peter 3:12, KJV: Looking for and **hasting** unto the coming of the day of God, wherein the heavens being on fire shall be dissolved, and the elements shall melt with fervent heat?*

The believers hasten the day of the God. **"Hasting"** is the Greek word **"speudo"** from where we get our English word **"speed."** We speed the coming of the day of God, and, according to Paul and Peter, this "speed" is linked to our lifestyle. Thus, the "end" is linked to believers. With that said, I will now develop "the end" (Habakkuk 2:3) at which the vision shall speak. I will do this from the Hebrew word pictures[16].

Hebrew words, Hawaiian words, Chinese words, ancient Egyptian words, and so on are made up of putting pictures together (hieroglyphic). For example, the Hebrew letter "b" (ב), pronounced as (beth) is derived from a picture of a "house" and

---

[15]See the NU texts. However, the M texts write it as a verb indicative aorist active 3rd person singular. The aorist tense also refers to an action that happened with ongoing results.
[16]Note: Hebrew word pictures ("HWP") are not to replace the inspired words of the Bible. HWP is used to clarify difficult words

"beth" in the Hebrew language means "house" (i.e., Beth-el—house of God).

The Hebrew word for "at the end" (Habakkuk 2:3) is "laqeets"(קֵץ),[17] which means "extremity." To provide an easy way to understand the hieroglyphic of "extremity," I will first discuss the letter "qoph" (ק) (Eng., "q"). "qoph" (ק), as indicated, means "behind," "the last," "the least." The Hebrew picture used to develop "qoph" (ק) is a picture of the back of the head. Hence, it means "behind" as the back, "last" as being in the back, etc. Thus, one can see why this letter is used in the word for "end" (קֵץ).

The next letter in the word for "end" is "tsadik" (צ). This letter means "a fishhook," "catch," "desire," "need," and "righteous (upright) man." With reference to this chapter, I will use the word picture of "a righteous man."

"Tsadik" is also linked to Melchizedek—"And Melchizedek (Heb., Malkiy-Tsedeq) king of Salem brought forth bread and wine: and he was the priest of the most high God" (Genesis 14:18, KJV).

"Lamed" (ל) is used as a prefix meaning "towards." However, "lamed's" word picture is that of a shepherd's staff. The meaning of this letter is that of "control," "authority," "the tongue," and so on. When it is used in front of a word it means "towards." Thus "at the end" could also read "towards the end."

If you have followed me so far, the Hebrew word picture for the phrase "the end" can mean: "the end" (קֵץ) happens at the

---

[17]Hebrew words are read and written from right to left.

"authority" (ל) of the "last" (ק) "tsadik" (צ) (the Melchizedek order). Let us put the word pictures[18] together. "The vision is …for the Congregation and towards the authority of the last Melchizedek order He shall speak."

If you can receive it, the vision is "yet for" His "congregation" "duplicating" the "order" of Melchizedek. In other words, the end of the vision is the congregation duplicating Him, as we become the last "tsadik" in the earth, as Jesus is our first "tsadik."

There was the "first" Adam (Genesis 3:9). Jesus is the "last Adam "(I Corinthians 15:45). There is the "first" Melchizedek (Genesis 14:18). There is the "last" Melchizedek (Hebrews 7:15).

The application for the Church, as the "new (corporate) man," is that Jesus has becomes the Church's "first" Melchizedek. Jesus is made in the "likeness of Melchizedek" (Hebrews 7:15), and the Church bodily (the congregation) becomes the "last" order of the Melchizedek priesthood. This order is a Body of a "royal priesthood" – 1 Peter 2:9; Revelation 1:6; Revelation 4:4, Revelation 20:6, etc.

Thus, the "the end" is linked to the Melchizedek order of priesthood. It is linked "into" the congregation who has become that kingdom of priests. The end will come as the Church rules as kings and priests unto God. The vision is "toward the end" which will be made a reality in the last "tsadik" – righteous ones. "The vision … at the end it shall speak (lit., breath, blow with breath, puff)" (Habakkuk 2:3, KJV).

---

[18] Note: Word pictures are not considered as replacing the Hebrew definitions. It is used to provide a picture that may inspire clearer meanings.

The Hebrew word picture for the preceding quote could read, "The vision ... at the authority of the last tsadik (Melchizedek order of priests) shall blow." The truth of God's vision is going to be "born from above" in His royal priesthood by the "breath" of the Holy Spirit.

The authority of the King's domain will be "preached" as a witness in the habitable earth (Matthew 24:14). The true "Spirit-sound" will finally be "heard" through the priests of the Melchizedek order (compare John 3:8). This Melchizedek order is made up many components.

The order of eternal priesthood, the order of giving bread and wine, the order of blessing, the order of righteousness, the order of peace, the order of incense (prayers), the order of "all things" of prophecy, speaking in tongues with interpretation, psalms, teaching, revelation, the order in "the spirit," the order of ruling priests, the order of the indestructible life, the order of living "into the age," and so on. Melchizedek's order is becoming a working reality among the entire congregation who walk in the "order" of Jesus, our Melchizedek.

*Hebrews 7:17, NKJV: For He testifies: **"You are a priest forever according to the order (Gk., táxin)** of Melchizedek."*

*Luke 1:8-9, NKJV: [8]... while he was serving as priest before God in the **order (Gk., táxin)** of his division, [9]..., his lot fell to burn incense...*

*1 Corinthians 14:26; 39-40, NKJV: [26] ... Whenever you come together, each of you has a psalm, has a teaching, has a tongue, has a revelation, has an interpretation. Let all things be done for edification... [39] ... desire earnestly to prophesy, and do not forbid to speak with tongues. [40] Let all things be done decently and in **order (Gk., táxin).***

*Colossians 2:5, NKJV: 5...I am with you in spirit (lit., the spirit), rejoicing to see your good **order (Gk., táxin)** and the steadfastness of your faith in Christ.*

*Revelation 20:6, NKJV: Blessed and holy is he who has part in the first resurrection. Over such the second death has no power, but they shall be **priests** of God and of Christ and shall **reign** with Him a thousand years.*

*1 Peter 2:9, NKJV: But you are a chosen generation, a **royal priesthood**, a holy nation...*

The verses above depict some of the aspects of the order of the Melchizedek priesthood. At the end, the last order of Melchizedek will be the authority in the earth. The vision will "speak." Saying it another way, the vision will become real.

His Vision Personified

Matthew 11:13-14, NKJV: ¹³*For all the prophets and the law prophesied until John.* ¹⁴*And if you are willing to receive it, he is Elijah who is to come.*

Habakkuk 2:3, NKJV: For the vision ... will surely come....

Hebrews 10:1, NKJV: For the law, having a shadow of the good things to come, and not the very image of the things, can never with these same sacrifices, which they offer continually year by year, make those who approach perfect.

Acts 12:9, NKJV: So, he went out and followed him, and did not know that what was done by the angel was real, but thought he was seeing a vision.

God's prophets and His law prophesied His vision until John, the Baptist. That is, the prophets only envisioned what was to be. The prophets before John, the Baptist did not experience the other real "Elijah who was to come."

Malachi 4:5, KJV Behold, I will send you Elijah the prophet before the coming of the great and dreadful day of the LORD:

Malachi's vision (prophesy) of "Elijah ... to come" was later personified (made real) in John, the Baptist. In the case of John, the Baptist, Malachi saw a vision of the Elijah "who is to come." When John the Baptist arrived, he was the reality of Malachi's vision.

John was that Elijah personified (Matthew 11:14). The Scripture was in the prophetic mode (vision mode) until John came and personified the prophecy. Can you see this?

Habakkuk also stated, "The vision ... will surely come." This "vision" that will "surely come" was also personified in Jesus. The same thing is true for "the law" with respect to Jesus. The law also prophesied until Jesus came.

The book of Hebrews says it this way: The law was a "shadow" (a reflection of the real) and "not the very image (reality) of the things." Jesus is the person (the very "body") of the shadow (law) (Hebrews 10:1; 10).

 John the Baptist is also the very image of prophesy or the reality of Malachi's vision. As indicated in a previous chapter, vision is not the "real" thing. His vision for your life is a prophecy until "your" John becomes real in your life. The writer of the book of Acts distinguished between realty and vision.

*Acts 12:9, NKJV: So, he went out and followed him, and did not know that what was done by the angel was **real**, but thought he was seeing a **vision.***

The fact of Acts 12:9 should be taught to the Church repeatedly (see Philippians 3:1). Vision is not real, until the vision come to pass. The congregation must not be kept in a "vision mode," so to speak. The Assembly of God (His Church) must be moved to a "place" called "real." Allow me to use Abraham to explain.

God evaluated Abraham by asking him to sacrifice his son. First, God told him of the place (Genesis 22:2). Abraham then "went to the place" (Genesis 22:3). On the third day, Abraham "saw the place" (Genesis 22:4). Finally, "They came to the place which God had told him" (Genesis 22:9).

First, God's instruction to Abraham was only a mental vision. He then began to walk in that mental instruction. Finally, the words of God to him became "real" — Abraham "came to the place." The point: there is a difference between vision (mental sight) and reality — the vision is no longer hidden.

The vision is now "real." The vision has now "come." The vision is now personified. John the Baptist (the promises of God to parents and their children) "will surely come." The same is true for our King. It will not always be a vision. His coming will not always be a prophecy. "He who is coming will come..." (Hebrews 10:37). "Is coming" is in present tense and middle voice in the Greek. "Will come" is future tense and active voice in the Greek text. If you can receive it: King Jesus "is coming," now, in His Church and He "will come."

Matthew 2:1-6, NKJV: ¹Now after Jesus was born in Bethlehem of Judea in the days of Herod the king, behold, wise men from the East came to Jerusalem, ²saying, "Where is He who has been born King of the Jews? For we have seen His star in the East and have come to worship Him." ³When Herod the king heard this, he was troubled, and all Jerusalem with him. ⁴And when he had gathered all the chief priests and scribes of the people together, he inquired of them where the Christ was to be born. ⁵So they said to him, "In Bethlehem of Judea, for thus it is written by the prophet. ⁶'But you, Bethlehem, in the land of Judah, are not the least among the rulers of Judah; for out of you shall come a Ruler, Who will shepherd My people Israel.' "

The Scriptures testified of Jesus long before He came physically (John 5:39, I Peter 1:10-11). In the words of our Lord, the law and the prophets prophesied until John. However, the reality of King Jesus came through His birth. His star appeared the day He was born, and the sad thing about this is that the religious people did not know that He was born.

It took wise men from the east to tell religious people of Jesus' real existence. The time came when the vision of Jesus' coming came to pass. When Jesus arrived on the scene, He was real. He was no longer a vision. The coming One came, the coming One is coming, and the coming One will come again. In fact, He was "born King…" the first time, and He is still King now! With that said, the vision is also for the congregation as we learned earlier. The congregation will fulfill the vision of Jesus for His Church. Part of the Vision of Jesus is for His Church to "apply His knowledge" in order to bring nations to God (Matthew 28:18-20; Matthew 24:14). His vision must be applied (personified) in the earth.

Ephesians 4:11-13: ¹¹And He Himself gave some to be apostles, some prophets, some evangelists, and some pastors and teachers, ¹²for the equipping of the saints for the work of ministry, for the edifying of the body of Christ, 13 till we all come to the unity of the faith and of the knowledge of the Son of God, to a perfect man, to the measure of the stature of the fullness of Christ.

Part of the vision of Jesus is for His apostles, prophets, teachers, evangelist, and pastors to mature the congregation to the place of "applying God's knowledge" in their lives. The Bible calls it the "work of the ministry." I asked the Lord what is the "work of the ministry?"

As I was meditating, I heard the words saying that "work is applied knowledge." Now, I am aware of the scientific definition of work (force multiplied by distance); and the ordinary definition such as occupation.

However, why does an employer employ a person for a job? Part of the reason is that the employee has the knowledge base to perform the job. Hence, during a workday, the employee is applying knowledge to complete a task. We call this process "work."

The purpose for the Church to "come to … the knowledge of the Son of God" is to do the "work of ministry." "Work of ministry" is applying the "knowledge of the Son of God" in "the deaconate" to demonstrate the "reality" of Jesus.

In other words, the Church has been saying for too long that we are going to do the "greater works" that Jesus prophesied. The congregation must now make His vision of greater works true. We must do and not just say! The congregation must "apply" the "knowledge" of God's reality to everyday life. His vision must be personified in us and through us. Vision must become a reality.

Tell the Vision to no One!

*Matthew 17:1-2; 5; 9, NKJV: ¹Now after six days Jesus took Peter, James, and John his brother, led them up on a high mountain by themselves; ²and He was transfigured before them. His face shone like the sun, and His clothes became as white as the light... ⁵...and suddenly a voice came out of the cloud, saying, "This is My Beloved Son, in whom I am well pleased. Hear Him! ...⁹Now as they came down from the mountain, Jesus commanded them, saying, "**Tell the vision to no one until** the Son of Man is risen from the dead."*

Jesus gave a directive: "Tell the vision to no one." Was this a permanent directive? The answer is no! Yet, why are we still not teaching the true significance of this vision? Or are some not telling the vision because some do not understand the full implication of this vision.

We must "consider the matter and understand the vision" (compare Daniel 9:23). After understanding comes, which is available after the third day (Jesus' resurrection day), we are obligated to "tell the vision," as Peter did (Matthew 17:9). Peter understood this vision to exemplify Jesus' "coming." Peter received this understanding from Jesus' statement to His disciples prior to His transfiguration.

Matthew 16:28-17:2, NKJV: ¹⁶:²⁸Assuredly, I say to you, there are some standing here who shall not taste death till they see the Son of Man coming in His kingdom. ¹⁷:¹Now after six days Jesus took Peter, James, and John his brother, led them up on a high mountain by themselves; ¹⁷:²and He was transfigured before them...

2 Peter 1:16-18, NKJV: ¹⁶For we did not follow cunningly devised fables when we made known to you the power and coming of our Lord Jesus Christ, but were eyewitnesses of His majesty (Gk., megaleióteetos). [17]*For He received from God the Father honor and glory when such a voice came to Him from the Excellent Glory: "This is My Beloved Son, in whom I am well pleased."* [18]*And we heard this voice which came from heaven when we were with Him on the holy mountain.*

Peter defined the Lord's transfiguration on the mountain as the Lord's "coming." Peter, James, and John were the "some … who shall not taste death till they see the Son of Man coming." This is significant, because the "vision" of Jesus' "transfiguration" happened on the earth at mountain top level, directly after Matthew 16:28.

Again, this happened before Jesus was crucified. This happened before the three (Peter James and John) died, and the Lord and Peter called the transfiguration Jesus' "coming." So, what does it really mean when the Scripture discusses the "coming of the Lord?"[19]

When He came (or was transfigured) on the mountain, He did not drop out of the sky. This transfiguration occurred "as He prayed." Luke 9:29, NKJV says, "And as He prayed, the appearance of His face was altered, and His robe became white and glistening."

Thus, a prayer life is significant relative to being transformed like Jesus. The Scripture teaches that we can be transformed like

---

[19]There is the coming of the Lord physically as He went up to heaven; and there is a coming of the Lord "in" His Saints. The Bible never said that the Lord would come "for" us. However, the Bible does say that the Lord will come "in" His Saints; and He will come "with" all His Saints.

Jesus right here on this earth by beholding the Lord's glory, by renewing our mind, and by "'inwrought' prayer."

Peter also equated the Lord's transfiguration to "majesty." "Majesty" is the Greek word "megaleióteetos" which also means "big." The emphasis of today is "mega Churches." However, is anyone telling the vision of "mega transfiguration?"

In other words, part of Jesus' vision is to emphasize the "mega" — bigness — of being transfigured on this earth. Peter called Jesus' coming on the mountain "megaleióteetos." His coming is "big."

His transfiguration is "big." His healing power is "big." What are we calling "mega?" There are three things that are called "megaleióteetos" in the Scripture.

One is found in Luke 9:43 where Jesus performed a "megaleióteetos" act after His transfiguration. In Luke 9:37-43, Jesus cast out an unclean spirit, which act the Bible called the "mighty power" of God (KJV) or "majesty" of God (NKJV). The Greek word for "mighty power" or "majesty" is "megaleióteetos."

The second place is 2 Peter1:16, cited earlier in this chapter. Peter was an eyewitness of Jesus' "megaleióteetos" transformation. The third place "megaleióteetos" is used is in Acts 19:27 referring to the man made "temple" of the "great goddess Diane...and her magnificence (Gk., megaleióteetos)." The "gathering" concerning this incident in Acts 19:20-41 is called an "assembly," which translates literally as "church" (Acts 19:41).

Thus, this "mob" represents assemblies that are really one of the "daughters" mystery Babylon (Revelation 17:5; Revelation 18:7).

Mystery Babylon is also a queen-mother who emphasizes "mega-temples (Churches). They also emphasize mega luxury, and so on.

The vision of most focuses more on the mega-temples which men are also calling "mega-churches." Contrarily, the apostolic vision of "mega" is the bigness of transfiguration and the bigness of casting out stubborn unclean spirits.

I am not doing away with big buildings (the sheep need sheep sheds). I also understand that vision not only includes the "whosoever" (Jesus and His people). Vision also involves, the "'whatsoever' (inanimate things) that are born out of God (I John 5:1; 4).

However, the vision is to become "mega" in His transfigured power. Most leaders have not personified, as they ought, the "mega" vision. They have not published this great truth after His resurrection.

Jesus did not say, "'forever' do not tell the vision of His mega-transfiguration." He said we could tell the vision after His resurrection. Men are refusing to "tell the vision." They are telling every other vision, except for the vision of His transfiguration.

According to Daniel and the book of Revelations, the Church is also to make this vision of transfiguration "real," before Jesus comes back physically. Yes! Jesus will come again the same way he went up (Acts 1:9-11).

Yet, the same Bible teaches that Jesus will come as the "early and latter rain" on the third day (see Hosea and James). The same Bible also teaches that He will also "come to be glorified in His saints" (2 Thessalonians 1:10a). What does "in" mean? "In" means "in," like "inside."

Jesus indeed comes to be glorified "in" the saints (Colossians 1:27; 2 Thessalonians 2:14); He will also come the same way He went up—a cloud under Him (Acts 1:9-11). The "cloud received" him. "Received" is the Greek word hupélaben which literally means to "receive under." The cloud "received" Jesus "under" it.

With that said, in His ascension the disciples saw Him ascend literally to which the angel says, "He will come again the same way"—upon a cloud or a cloud under Him. According to the book of Hebrews, "cloud(s)" is also a symbol of Saints.

If you can receive this, Jesus will also come in a cloud. His coming, as outlined by Paul in 2 Thessalonians 1:10, is internal. His appearing "in" us is His coming in a cloud.

The Bible indicates that the Son of man will come "with clouds," "with all His saints," "upon clouds" and "in a cloud," in His saints (Mark 14:62; 1 Thessalonians 3:13Matthew 24:30; Luke 21:27).

There is a coming of Jesus on the "inside" of His Saints ("in a cloud"), and He will eventually descend "with all His Saints" (clouds under Him, clouds amidst Him, or He upon the clouds).

His vision for us also includes a mega-transfiguration from the inside. In the words of Paul, Jesus will also "come to be glorified in His saints" (2 Thessalonians 1:10a). Jesus' appearing in us is also to birth the "first-fruits Christ," the first to become like Jesus in every way.

Historically, the first partakers of Jesus' transfiguration are the "three" disciples "taken"[20] by Jesus with Him to the Mount; they represent the Peters, the James, and the Johns of today. This vision is for the "Church of the firstborns"— those who "produce" (birth) this vision "first."

This transfiguration is available to anyone who presses into being "taken" and "changed." This change is not just available to an elite group of believers. The opportunity is for all who decides to fulfill Philippians 3:10-15 and Philippians 3:21. This "change" is the reality of His glory revealed from within us (2 Corinthians 3:17-18). Peter called this glory "megaleióteetos" — "big."

Hence, what I have called the fulfillment of true "mega-vision." This is similar to the vision that Daniel called a "great vision." The vision of being transfigured into "a united man;" which means, we get to look like Jesus as He was transfigured.

It is a little easier to believe for forgiveness than to believe that the cripple can be transfigured into a walking man (Luke 5:23). It follows that it is a little easier to believe for mega-churches of forgiven people than to believe for "mega-transfiguration" — the Church of the firstborns who allows Jesus to make "transfigured life" a reality in them.

Let us continue to trust God for both Church growths by forgiveness and the power to transform our apparent paralysis, as Jesus did with the crippled man, with the understanding that transfiguration is also glorious.

---

[20]Compare Enoch who was taken by God so that he did not see death

Transfiguration is "bigger." You will hear God's voice saying some similar things to you as He told Jesus at His transfiguration—"This is My beloved Son." You will hear Him say you are "accepted in the Beloved" (see Ephesians 1:6). How do I know this?

Ephesians 1:3b says we are "blessed" (lit., eulogy (to speak well of) with every spiritual blessing in the heavenly places in Christ." The Lord has spoken well over us, and He will yet speak well over us by transfiguring us into Jesus' glorious image. The vision of transfiguration must become a reality in the firstborns.

Eagle Flight

*Revelation 8:13, NASU: ... I heard an **eagle**[21] flying in midheaven, saying with a loud voice, "Woe, woe, woe.*

*Revelation 4:7d, NASU: ...the fourth creature was like a **flying eagle**.*

The Lord Jesus directed me December 31, 2000, to merge the Church I was overseeing with another ministry[22] for a specific time. He impressed upon me through the written Word (by revelation) that doing this was as Abraham giving up his only son. I did do the desire of the Father as He had requested. That night, as I sought the Father to "make sure" I was hearing correctly, a vision broke through to me.

I saw a great eagle standing up with its wings raised for flight in the middle of a building of the Church I was to merge with. This eagle was made up of people. As I looked, I saw the eagle being completed. The right wing grew with people to its full length.

It appeared as if people were added to the wing as a hand fan opening. After the growth of the wing, the eagle began to lift by extending its wings for flight. I then heard a voice say, "From this I will launch you to the nations."

In the early 1990s, I also saw another eagle made of what appeared to be sculptured and old looking limestone. It was poised on the edge of the border of Germany, spreading its wings to take flight. The flight was a flight of war towards America (I knew it was a flight of war because I heard the

---

[21]The Greek Texts (NU) and the Majority Texts read "eagle" as translated in the NASU, NIV, ASV and RSV.
[22]This ministry is Sandra Hayden Ministries

words). However, the Chancellor counseled the government not to do it at the time.

Around 1988, I saw another huge eagle in flight high in the clouds. The color of the eagle was as the flag of the United States of America. The eagle was large and majestic as it flew with focus and confidence. It was a magnificent sight. As the eagle was flying, I heard the "sound" of thunders. As I continued to listen, the "sounds" of the thunder became a "voice" of thunder. I heard the voice of thunder say, "Judgment, judgment, judgment…"

At the time of the vision of the flying eagle in which I heard the voice of thunder, I was young in the Lord ("a son" of two or three years) and did not understand the vision (compare Daniel 8:27, last part). I asked my Pastor at that time what the vision meant. He did not know!

In fact, no one knew what the vision meant, except for one lady. Her response to me was that "the vision is ministry…," "the vision is ministry." Thus, I asked a logical question. What is "ministry," as it relates to a flying eagle or an eagle flying?

Revelation 4:7-8, NKJV: 7 … the fourth living creature was like a flying eagle. 8 … And they do not rest day or night, saying: "Holy, holy, holy.

The "flying eagle" is also one of God's worshippers among the living creatures! For those who have any ministry, one of the first orders of business is worshiping the Lord in flight (the heavenly place). We must remain ascended in the flight of worship. The "flying eagle," along with the rest of the living creatures, did "not rest day and night, saying: Holy, holy, holy…"

Jesus said we are to begin our prayers by saying, "Our Father, holy is your Name" (see Matthew 6:9). The command is to start our prayer by recognizing the father's Holiness, or the holiness of His fatherhood. We must mount up at His "command." We must mount with "holy, holy, holy is the Lord God Almighty ...." in our mouths. Or "'dreadful, dreadful, dreadful' is the Lord God Almighty ...." As we worship according to His commands, we will make our "nest (place of rest) on high."

*Job 39:27, NKJV: Does **the eagle** mount up at your command, and make its nest on high?*

Obeying His command (lit., mouth) will cause us to make our "nest on high." In other words, worshiping the Lord by declaring His awesomeness will cause us to remain in the heavenly place.

In Revelation 8:13, the eagle flew in "mid-heaven." Paul's goal was also that upward calling of God, the place where he could peer about in God. "I (Paul) press toward the goal (lit., to scope, to peer about) for the prize of the upward call of God in Christ Jesus" (Philippians 3:14, NKJV).

The Apostle, John recorded Jesus' declaration of the life of "true worship" and "Spirit worship" (John 4). With that said, it is also important to note that there are four cherubs in Ezekiel and Revelation.

Each one of these cherubs could correspond to one of the four gospels. The fourth cherub in Ezekiel's and John's writing (Revelation) is that of an eagle or a flying eagle. Thus, the gospel of John (fourth in the series of gospels) appears to be the book that corresponds to the eagle or the flying eagle (fourth in the list of cherubs).

Yes, the lion (Judah) is also a symbol of worship that destroys the enemy (Genesis 49). Yet, the flying eagle is a symbol of those who worship in the Spirit (the heavenly Wind of God) and in the Truth (not hidden like a conspicuous eagle in flight with the Holy Spirit under its wings). In addition to the height of worship, the flying eagle also has another role — the flying eagle relates to the trumpet.

Hosea 8:1, NKJV: Set the trumpet to your mouth! He shall come[23] like ***an eagle*** *against the house of the LORD....*

Revelation 8:13, NASU: Then I looked, and I heard ***an eagle[24]*** *flying in midheaven, saying with a loud voice, "Woe, woe, woe to those who dwell on the earth, because of the remaining blasts of the trumpet of the three angels who are about to sound!"*

Hosea 8:1 cited above should read as follows: **"Set the trumpet to your mouth! ...like an eagle..."** The translators added the additional phrase — **"he shall come"** — translators periodically add their clarifications to some Scriptures. I am glad they were courteous enough to put their additions in "italics," to keep us informed of the changes.

Nonetheless, Hosea 8:1 indicates that the eagle's cry is as a trumpet to the mouth. Thus, the eagle is associated with a trumpet. The New Testament also links the eagle with the trumpet, as seen in the book of Revelation.

Revelation 8:13 stated that a flying eagle warned of the trumpet blasts to be sounded. The eagle cried with a loud voice, "Woe,

---

[23]The phrase "he shall come" is not in the Hebrew text. This phrase was supplied by the translator. Hence it is italicized in most translations
[24]The Greek texts—the Alexandrian Text (NU) and the Majority Texts— read "eagle" as translated in the NASU, NIV, ASV and RSV.

woe, woe to those who dwell on the earth, because of the remaining blasts (lit., voices, or sounds) of the trumpet..." One of the symbols of the trumpet is that of a prophet who is a watchman, or one who "overlays" the saints in prayer.

*Ezekiel 33:1-3; 7, NKJV: ¹ Again the word of the LORD came to me, saying, ² ... 'When I bring the sword upon a land, and the people of the land take a man from their territory and make him their **watchman,** ³ when he sees the sword coming upon the land, if he **blows** the **trumpet** and warns the people ... ⁷"**So you,** son of man: I have made you a watchman for the house of Israel; therefore, you shall hear a word from My mouth and **warn** them for Me.*

As one can see, the prophetic watchman is that person who blows the trumpet. God's "word" from His mouth is equated to the prophet seeing into God and blowing the trumpet as he sees and hears from God. Thus, the eagle's cry, referring to its voice being like a trumpet, is the prophetic warning from the sight, hearing and cry imparted in it by the Spirit of Jesus.

The word "watchman" used in Ezekiel 33, also means "covering," "to lean forward" and "to peer into the distance' (see Strong's Concordance). Thus, like the eagle with "far sight," apostolic and prophetic seers can give warnings from God. Their "eyes observe" far "into the distance;" especially those who "overlays" the saints in prayer.

*Job 39:27-29, NKJV: ²⁷Does the eagle **mount up** at your command, And make its nest on high? ²⁸On the rocks it dwells and resides, On the crag of the rock and the stronghold. ²⁹From there it spies (lit., pry into) out the prey (lit., food); Its eyes observe (lit., scan) from afar.*

It is from the high places of mid-heaven and cliffs of the rocks that eagles "scan" into God's distant plans. They observe God's "food" (God's "will" to reap the harvest, according to Jesus), and they declare God's Words. They fly high and see deep, deep into the deep things of God and they go for the things of God as for "prey" — food.

In Revelation 8:13, the flying eagle "spied" out three "woes" from "mid-heaven." As this eagle flew, seeing the effect of the distant trumpets, it declared the three "woes." There will be change in the function of the church. She will become a prophetic declarer of woes (Revelation 11:1-10, Acts 24:5, Acts 17:6, etc.).

Revelation 8:13, NASU: Then I looked, and I heard an eagle[25] flying in midheaven, saying with a loud voice, "Woe, woe, woe ...

*Ezekiel 2:9-10, NKJV: [9]Now when I looked, there was a hand stretched out to me; and behold, a scroll of a book was in it... [10]and written on it were lamentations (lit., dirge songs, to beat the chest in wailing) and mourning (lit., mutter, **rumble (as thunder)** ponder, complain, and woe (lit., groans).*

The flying eagle in Revelation declared "woe" — "an interjection (expression) of grief or of denunciation" (Thayer). The prophet (Ezekiel) was assigned to also speak "woe" (rt., groan). The point: The Body of Christ and the world should brace themselves for the heavenly eagles that are flying with woe in their mouth. They are warning of the trumpets which are blowing (compare Revelation 11:1-13). They will also "Set the trumpet to [their] mouth! ...like an eagle..."

---

[25]As previously indicated, the Greek texts, the Alexandrian Text (NU) and the Majority Texts read "eagle" as translated in the NASU, NIV, ASV and RSV

In conclusion, the eagle is foremost a symbol of our resurrected (living) King who ascended to the heavens. The Hebrew word for eagle "naasher" comes from a root that means to lacerate. "Naasher" (רשׁנ) is also associated with a base word that means "prince" "sar" (רשׂ), a picture of a devouring person, and from the Hebrew letter "noon" (נ). "Noon" ("n") depicts a picture of a fish, life, activity, seed, posterity, continue, etc.

Thus, the word for eagle also means the "prince who fishes" (Jesus the evangelist), the "living prince" (Jesus being resurrected) the "active prince" (Holy Spirit Power). Again, who is this "Living Prince?" His name is Jesus. He is that Prince who lives in us. He is the "life" giving "Prince" (Revelation 1:5, 1 Corinthians 15:45). Jesus is the "Prince of Peace" who ascended on High.

Ephesians 4:8-10, NKJV: ⁸Therefore He says: "When He ascended on high, He led captivity captive, and gave gifts to men." ⁹(Now this, "He ascended" – what does it mean but that He also first descended into the lower parts of the earth? ¹⁰ He who descended is also the One who ascended far above all the heavens, that He might fill all things.).

Our living King divided himself into five "Christ's gifts" (Ephesians 4:7). He "gave gifts to men" when He ascended to His Heavenly Nest or Throne. Thus, when He ascended His anointing remained on the earth with each of the five gifts having a certain "measure" of His anointing (Ephesians 4:7). Ephesians 4:11 names these gifts as: apostles, prophets, evangelists, pastors, and teachers.

Each of these gifts has a "measure of Christ's gift" (Ephesians 4:7). These gifts are related to His ascension as the Eagle – the life-giving King or the Prince who fishes. When He ascended on high, He ... gave gifts to men." One of the purposes of these gifts is to mature the Body of Christ to that ascended state of being.

Saying it another way, moving from vision to flight, part of the emphasis of competent and mature men/women of God should be to train the called to do the "work of the ministry" from a heavenly view (part of which is to become fishers of men) (Ephesians 2:6; Philippians 3:20; Luke 5:10; Mark 1:17).

This work of the ministry also includes the saints also supplying their "measure." In the vision, I saw at the end of the year 2000, the eagle was made up of people (plural). Thus, each person supplied their measure at their assigned place in this corporate eagle. Ephesians states that the purpose of the five-fold ministries is to bring the saints unto that perfect[26] (complete extension like a telescope) man—"the measure of the stature of the fullness of Christ" (Ephesians 4:13, NKJV).

A teacher can only bring a disciple to the same height or measure as the teacher. "It is enough for a disciple that he be like his teacher..." (Matthew 10:25, NKJV). Thus, the five-fold ministries must bring those who are called to a place of walking competently in the Spirit of Jesus. We are to build competent prophetic administrators. The Church now needs "skilled" harvesters. Listen to the cry of our Living King.

Luke 10:1-2, NKJV: ¹*...the Lord appointed seventy others also, and* **sent (Gk., apostello)** *them two by two before His face...* ²*Then He said to them, "The harvest truly is great, but the laborers are few;*

---

[26]One facet of "perfection," according to Hebrews 10:1-2, is not being conscious of any past sins that have been removed by Jesus' blood through His forgiveness.

therefore, pray the Lord of the harvest to send *(Gk.: ekballo, to throw out)* out laborers into His harvest.

Mark 1:12, NKJV: And immediately the Spirit drove (lit., ekballo, to throw out) Him [Jesus] into the wilderness.

"The laborers are few" and like the eagle that eventually must "throw out" its maturing offspring into flight, so our heavenly Eagle (the living King) shall "send (throw out)" those who are able to fly into His work of the ministry (Deuteronomy 32:11-12).

There are some things that the Spirit must "drive" us to do. The Spirit "drove" Jesus into a forty day fast in the wilderness (see Mark 1:12 above). Walking in the Spirit sometimes means to be "driven" by the Holy Spirit. Training for "flight" – the work of the ministry – should not take forever.

I understand that preparation of the seven angels to sound the seven trumpets may be as long twenty-one years (Revelation 8). However, sometimes we must be driven to expedite the process! Jesus trained twelve apostles in approximately three-and-a half years.

So, why do most men in the name of "their" vision want to hold and control people all their lives. The living King is opposite. He wants to throw out laborers into the harvest.

It is the season of the flying eagles. It is the season to train and release the mature eagles. Those who can spot fishes ("every kind") in the sea of humanity from high above (this is a heavenly prophetic vision) – John 4:16-19 w/4:25.

Then the eagles with agility, speed and accuracy harvest the fishes from the water while in flight (vision reality) — John 4:35-39. Saying it another way, we must mature competent prophetic ministers and other leaders through His vision, agility, speed, exactness, and realness. We must mature the potential leaders with "speed" by discipleship, as Jesus did the twelve to go forward and gather/separate crops for the Lord of the harvest

In other words, maturity (a goal of vision) cannot be expedited (becomes a reality) unless we disciple the saints and leaders by the Holy Spirit, by Word, by doctrine, with personal interacting, by friendship, by righteousness, by romping, by fasting, by love, by correction, by giving, by eating together, by example, by mutual respect, etc.

It takes more than Sunday, more than the false idea of "tithing-up" and more than a classroom setting to expedite maturity (this is primarily for those who learn from a distance and have no personal relationship with father ministries and/or fathers who have turned their hearts to the children). A result of Jesus' vision becoming real is "keen" harvesters.

Like the eagle that watch over their young (Mark 9:16), with personal relationships until the time of their flight — ministry, let us mature by genuine relationship those who show the seal of following Jesus, those who are willing to aggressively pursue the Lord Jesus' character. Let Jesus' vision of us becoming "as He is" grow to be real in us — **Vision Real.**

By Donald Peart, called a son by the Father

OTHER BOOKS

Poiema, by Judith Peart
Wisdom from Above, by Judith Peart
Procreation, Understanding Sex, and Identity, by Judith Peart
100 Nevers, by Judith Peart
The Shattered and the Healing by Judith Peart

The Lamb, by Donald Peart
Jesus' Resurrection, Our Inheritance, by Donald Peart.
Sexuality, By Donald Peart
Forgiven 490, by Donald Peart w/Judith Peart!
The Days of the Seventh Angel, By Donald Peart
The Torah (The Principle) of Giving, by Donald Peart
The Time Came, by Donald Peart
The Last Hour, the First Hour, the Forty-Second Generation, by Donald Peart
Vision Real, by Donald Peart
The False Prophet, Alias, Another Beast V1, by Donald Peart
"the beast," by Donald Peart
Son of Man Prophesy Against the false prophet, by Donald Peart
The Dragon's Tail, Prophets who Teach Lies, by Donald Peart
The Work of Lawlessness Revealed, by Donald Peart
When the Lord Made the Tempter, by Donald Peart
Examining Doctrine, Volume 1, by Donald Peart
Exousia, Your God Given Authority, by Donald Peart
The Numbers of God, by Donald Peart
The Completions of the Ages, the Gate, the Door, and the Veil, by Donald Peart
The Revelation of Jesus Christ, by Donald Peart
Jude—Translation and Commentary, by Donald Peart
Obtaining the Better Resurrection, by Donald Peart
Manifestations from Our Lord Jesus Christ as documented by Donald and Judith Peart
The New Testament, Dr. Donald Peart Exegesis

The Tree of Life, By Dr. Donald Peart
The Spirit and Power of John, the Baptist by Donald Peart
The Shattered and the Healing by Judith Peart
The Ugliest Man God Made by Donald Peart
Does Answering the Call of God Impact Your Children? by Donald Peart
Victory Out-of-the Beast-the Harvest of the Earth by Donald Peart
The Order of Melchizedek by Donald Peart
Ezekiel-the House-the City-the Land (Interpreting the Patterns) by Donald Peart
Butter and Honey, Understanding how to Choose the Good and Refuse Evil, by Donald Peart

CONTACT INFORMATION:
Crown of Glory Ministries
P.O. Box 1041 Randallstown, MD 21133
donaldpeart7@gmail.com

About the Author:
Donald Peart is married to Judith Peart since 1986. They believe that Jesus is the Christ, the Son of the living God; and they preach the gospel of God's kingdom centered on Jesus Christ. They have founded and currently oversee Crown of Glory Ministries in Randallstown, Maryland. Donald and his wife have written over 35 books; and their ministry has distributed their books to at least 29 States in the USA and 21 countries. Donald has earned an Associate of Arts degree in Pre-Engineering, a Bachelor of Science degree in Civil Engineering. He also earned a Master of Divinity, a Master of Science in Construction Management, and a Doctorate in Theology.

www.ingramcontent.com/pod-product-compliance
Lightning Source LLC
Chambersburg PA
CBHW060423050426

42449CB00009B/2109